R
POET

This book includes the Rumi's
Poems

Translated by Rumi expert
BURHAN UNVER

Who was Rumi?

Maulana Jalaluddin Rumi was a 13th century Persian poet, an Islamic dervish and a Sufi mystic. He is regarded as one of the greatest spiritual masters and poetical intellects. Born in 1207 AD, he belonged to a family of learned theologians. He made use of everyday life's circumstances to describe the spiritual world. Rumi's poems have acquired immense popularity, especially among the Persian speakers of Afghanistan, Iran and Tajikistan. Numerous poems written by the great poet have been translated to different languages.

Rumi's father was Bahā ud-Dīn Walad, a scholar, legal adviser and a spiritualist from Balkh, who was additionally referred to by the adherents of Rumi as Sultan al-Ulama or "Sultan of the Scholars".The most imperative impacts upon Rumi, other than his father, were the Persian artists Attar and Sanai. Rumi communicates his appreciation: "Attar was the spirit, Sanai his eyes twain, And in time thereafter, Came we in their train"

He further appreciates the two in another sonnet: "Attar has traversed the seven cities of Love, We are still at the turn of one street".

Rumi's works are written mostly in Persian, but occasionally he also used Turkish, Arabic, and Greek in his verse. His Mathnawī, composed in Konya, is considered one of the greatest poems of the Persian language.

He is regarded as one of the most popular and accomplished poets of all times, and he has been best selling poet in the United States of America. Rumi's work is so relevant to the modern day world that it trends on internet even to this date.

A New Rule

It is the rule with drunkards to fall upon each other,
to quarrel, become violent, and make a scene.
The lover is even worse than a drunkard.
I will tell you what love is: to enter a mine of gold.
And what is that gold?
The lover is a king above all kings,
unafraid of death, not at all interested in a golden crown.
The dervish has a pearl concealed under his patched cloak.
Why should he go begging door to door?
Last night that moon came along,
drunk, dropping clothes in the street.
"Get up," I told my heart, "Give the soul a glass of wine.
The moment has come to join the nightingale in the garden,
to taste sugar with the soul-parrot."
I have fallen, with my heart shattered -
where else but on your path? And I
broke your bowl, drunk, my idol, so drunk,
don't let me be harmed, take my hand.
A new rule a new law has been born:
break all the glasses and fall toward the glassblower.

-Mewlana Jalaluddin Rumi

Behind The Scenes

Is it your face
that adorns the garden?
Is it your fragrance
that intoxicates this garden?
Is it your spirit
that has made this brook
a river of wine?
Hundreds have looked for you
and died searching
in this garden
where you hide behind the scenes.
But this pain is not for those
who come as lovers.
You are easy to find here.
You are in the breeze
and in this river of wine.

-Mewlana Jalaluddin Rumi

Defeated By Love

The sky was lit
by the splendor of the moon
So powerful
I fell to the ground
Your love
has made me sure
I am ready to forsake
this worldly life
and surrender
to the magnificence
of your Being

-Mewlana Jalaluddin Rumi

Draw It Now From Eternity's Jar

Come, come, awaken all true drunkards!
Pour the wine that is Life itself!
O cupbearer of the Eternal Wine,
Draw it now from Eternity's Jar!
This wine doesn't run down the throat
But it looses torrents of words!
Cupbearer, make my soul fragrant as musk,
This noble soul of mine that knows the Invisible!
Pour out the wine for the morning drinkers!
Pour them this subtle and priceless musk!
Pass it around to everyone in the assembly
In the cups of your blazing drunken eyes!
Pass a philter from your eyes to everyone else's
In a way the mouth knows nothing of,
For this is the way cupbearers always offer
The holy and mysterious wine to lovers.
Hurry, the eyes of every atom in Creation
Are famished for this flaming-out of splendour!
Procure for yourself this fragrance of musk
And with it split open the breast of heaven!
The waves of the fragrance of this musk
Drive all Josephs out of their minds forever!

-Mewlana Jalaluddin Rumi

Here I Am

All night, a man called 'Allah'
Until his lips were bleeding.
Then the Devil said, 'Hey! Mr Gullible!
How comes you've been calling all night
And never once heard Allah say, 'Here, I am'?
You call out so earnestly and, in reply, what?
I'll tell you what. Nothing!'

The man suddenly felt empty and abandoned.
Depressed, he threw himself on the ground
And fell into a deep sleep.
In a dream, he met Abraham, who asked,
'Why are you regretting praising Allah?'

The man said, ' I called and called
But Allah never replied, 'Here I am.'
Abraham explained, 'Allah has said,
'Your calling my name is My reply.
Your longing for Me is My message to you.
All your attempts to reach Me
Are in reality My attempts to reach you.
Your fear and love are a noose to catch Me.
In the silence surrounding every call of 'Allah'
Waits a thousand replies of 'Here I am.'

-Mewlana Jalaluddin Rumi

I Am And I Am Not

I'm drenched
in the flood
which has yet to come
I'm tied up
in the prison
which has yet to exist
Not having played
the game of chess
I'm already the checkmate
Not having tasted
a single cup of your wine
I'm already drunk
Not having entered
the battlefield
I'm already wounded and slain
I no longer
know the difference
between image and reality
Like the shadow
I am
And
I am not

-Mewlana Jalaluddin Rumi

I Am Part Of The Load

I am part of the load
Not rightly balanced
I drop off in the grass,
like the old Cave-sleepers, to browse
wherever I fall.

For hundreds of thousands of years I have been dust-grains
floating and flying in the will of the air,
often forgetting ever being
in that state, but in sleep
I migrate back. I spring loose
from the four-branched, time -and-space cross,
this waiting room.

I walk into a huge pasture
I nurse the milk of millennia

Everyone does this in different ways.
Knowing that conscious decisions
and personal memory
are much too small a place to live,
every human being streams at night
into the loving nowhere, or during the day,
in some absorbing work.

-Mewlana Jalaluddin Rumi

I Have a Fire for You in my Mouth

I have a fire for you in my mouth, but I have a hundred seals
on my tongue.
The flames which I have in my heart would make one mouth-
ful of both worlds.
Though the entire world should pass away, without the world
I possess the kingdom of a hundred worlds.
Caravans which are loaded with sugar I have in motion for
the Egypt of nonexistence.
The drunkenness of love makes me unaware whether I have
profit of loss therefrom.
The body's eye was scattering pearls because of love, till now
I have a pearl-scattering soul.
I am not housebound, for like Jesus I have a home in the fourth
Heaven.
Thanks be to Him who gives soul to the body; if the soul
should depart, yet I have the soul of the soul.
Seek from me that which Shams-e Tabrizi has bestowed, for
I have the same.

-Mewlana Jalaluddin Rumi

I have been tricked by flying too close

I have been tricked by flying too close
to what I thought I loved.
Now the candleflame is out, the wine spilled,
and the lovers have withdrawn
somewhere beyond my squinting.
The amount I thought I'd won, I've lost.
My prayers becomes bitter and all about blindness.
How wonderful it was to be for a while
with those who surrender.
Others only turn their faces on way,
then another, like pigeon in flight.
I have known pigeons who fly in a nowhere,
and birds that eat grainlessness,
and tailor who sew beautiful clothes
by tearing them to pieces.

-Mewlana Jalaluddin Rumi

I See so Deeply Within Myself

I see so deeply within myself.
Not needing my eyes, I can see everything clearly.
Why would I want to bother my eyes again
Now that I see the world through His eyes?

-Mewlana Jalaluddin Rumi

I Swear

I swear, since seeing Your face,
the whole world is fraud and fantasy
The garden is bewildered as to what is leaf
or blossom. The distracted birds
can't distinguish the birdseed from the snare.

A house of love with no limits,
a presence more beautiful than venus or the moon,
a beauty whose image fills the mirror of the heart.

-Mewlana Jalaluddin Rumi

I Throw It All Away

You play with the great globe of union,
you that see everyone so clearly
and cannot be seen. Even universal
intelligence gets blurry when it thinks
you may leave. You came here alone,
but you create hundreds of new worlds.
Spring is a peacock flirting with
revelation. The rose gardens flame.
Ocean enters the boat. I throw
it all away, except this love for Shams.

-Mewlana Jalaluddin Rumi

I was dead

i was dead
i came alive
i was tears
i became laughter

all because of love
when it arrived
my temporal life
from then on
changed to eternal

love said to me
you are not
crazy enough
you don't
fit this house

i went and
became crazy
crazy enough
to be in chains

love said
you are not
intoxicated enough
you don't
fit the group

i went and
got drunk
drunk enough
to overflow
with light-headedness

love said
you are still
too clever
filled with
imagination and skepticism

i went and
became gullible
and in fright
pulled away
from it all

love said
you are a candle
attracting everyone
gathering every one
around you

i am no more
a candle spreading light
i gather no more crowds
and like smoke
i am all scattered now

love said
you are a teacher
you are a head
and for everyone
you are a leader

i am no more
not a teacher
not a leader
just a servant
to your wishes

love said
you already have
your own wings
i will not give you
more feathers

and then my heart
pulled itself apart
and filled to the brim
with a new light
overflowed with fresh life

now even the heavens
are thankful that
because of love
i have become
the giver of light

-Mewlana Jalaluddin Rumi

If a Tree could Wander

Oh, if a tree could wander
and move with foot and wings!
It would not suffer the axe blows
and not the pain of saws!

For would the sun not wander
away in every night ?
How could at ev'ry morning
the world be lighted up?

And if the ocean's water
would not rise to the sky,
How would the plants be quickened
by streams and gentle rain?

The drop that left its homeland,
the sea, and then returned ?
It found an oyster waiting
and grew into a pearl.

Did Yusaf not leave his father,
in grief and tears and despair?
Did he not, by such a journey,
gain kingdom and fortune wide?

Did not the Prophet travel
to far Medina, friend?
And there he found a new kingdom
and ruled a hundred lands.

You lack a foot to travel?
Then journey into yourself!
And like a mine of rubies
receive the sunbeams? print!

Out of yourself ? such a journey
will lead you to your self,
It leads to transformation
of dust into pure gold!

-Mewlana Jalaluddin Rumi

If You Show Patience

If you show patience, I'll rid you of this virtue.
If you fall asleep, I'll rub the sleep from your eyes.
If you become a mountain, I'll melt you in fire.
And if you become an ocean, I'll drink all your water.

-Mewlana Jalaluddin Rumi

If you Want What Visible Reality

If you want what visible reality
can give, you're an employee.
If you want the unseen world,
you're not living your truth.
Both wishes are foolish,
but you'll be forgiven for forgetting
that what you really want is
love's confusing joy.

-Mewlana Jalaluddin Rumi

In Love

In love, aside from sipping the wine of timelessness,
nothing else exists.
There is no reason for living except for giving one's life.
I said, 'First I know you, then I die.'
He said, 'For the one who knows Me, there is no dying.'

-Mewlana Jalaluddin Rumi

In the End

In the end, the mountains of imagination were nothing
but a house.
And this grand life of mine was nothing but an excuse.
You've been hearing my story so patiently for a lifetime
Now hear this: it was nothing but a fairy tale.

-Mewlana Jalaluddin Rumi

In The Arc Of Your Mallet

Don't go anywhere without me.
Let nothing happen in the sky apart from me,
or on the ground, in this world or that world,
without my being in its happening.
Vision, see nothing I don't see.
Language, say nothing.
The way the night knows itself with the moon,
be that with me. Be the rose
nearest to the thorn that I am.
I want to feel myself in you when you taste food,
in the arc of your mallet when you work,
when you visit friends, when you go
up on the roof by yourself at night.
There's nothing worse than to walk out along the street
without you. I don't know where I'm going.
You're the road, and the knower of roads,
more than maps, more than love

-**Mewlana Jalaluddin Rumi**

Last night you left me and slept

Last night you left me and slept
your own deep sleep. Tonight you turn
and turn. I say,
"You and I will be together
till the universe dissolves."
You mumble back things you thought of
when you were drunk.

-Mewlana Jalaluddin Rumi

In the Waters of Purity

In the waters of purity, I melted like salt
Neither blasphemy, nor faith, nor conviction, nor
doubt remained.
In the center of my heart a star has appeared
And all the seven heavens have become lost in it.

-Mewlana Jalaluddin Rumi

Let go of your worries

Let go of your worries
and be completely clear-hearted,
like the face of a mirror
that contains no images.
If you want a clear mirror,
behold yourself
and see the shameless truth,
which the mirror reflects.
If metal can be polished
to a mirror-like finish,
what polishing might the mirror
of the heart require?
Between the mirror and the heart
is this single difference:
the heart conceals secrets,
while the mirror does not.

-Mewlana Jalaluddin Rumi

Late, by Myself

Late, by myself, in the boat of myself,
no light and no land anywhere,
cloudcover thick. I try to stay
just above the surface,
yet I'm already under
and living with the ocean

-Mewlana Jalaluddin Rumi

Light Breeze

As regards feeling pain, like a hand cut in battle,
consider the body a robe you wear.

When you meet someone you love, do you kiss their clothes?
Search out who's inside.

Union with God is sweeter than body comforts.

We have hands and feet different from these. Sometimes in
dream we see them.

That is not illusion. It's seeing truly. You do have a spirit
body;

don't dread leaving the physical one. Sometimes someone
feels this truth so strongly that he or she can live in mountain
solitude totally refreshed.

The worried, heroic doings of men and women seem weary
and futile to dervishes enjoying the light breeze of spirit.

-Mewlana Jalaluddin Rumi

Let Me Be Mad

O incomparable Giver of life, cut reason loose at last!
Let it wander grey-eyed from vanity to vanity.
Shatter open my skull, pour in it the wine of madness!
Let me be mad, as You; mad with You, with us.
Beyond the sanity of fools is a burning desert
Where Your sun is whirling in every atom:
Beloved, drag me there, let me roast in Perfection!

-Mewlana Jalaluddin Rumi

Like This

If anyone asks you
how the perfect satisfaction
of all our sexual wanting
will look, lift your face
and say,

Like this.

When someone mentions the gracefulness
of the nightsky, climb up on the roof
and dance and say,

Like this.

If anyone wants to know what "spirit" is,
or what "God's fragrance" means,
lean your head toward him or her.
Keep your face there close.

Like this.

When someone quotes the old poetic image
about clouds gradually uncovering the moon,
slowly loosen knot by knot the strings
of your robe.

Like this.

If anyone wonders how Jesus raised the dead,
don't try to explain the miracle.
Kiss me on the lips.

Like this. Like this.

When someone asks what it means
to "die for love," point
here.

If someone asks how tall I am, frown
and measure with your fingers the space
between the creases on your forehead.

This tall.

The soul sometimes leaves the body, the returns.
When someone doesn't believe that,
walk back into my house.

Like this.

When lovers moan,
they're telling our story.

Like this.

I am a sky where spirits live.
Stare into this deepening blue,
while the breeze says a secret.

Like this.

When someone asks what there is to do,
light the candle in his hand.

Like this.

How did Joseph's scent come to Jacob?

Huuuuu.

How did Jacob's sight return?

Huuuu.

A little wind cleans the eyes.

Like this.

When Shams comes back from Tabriz,
he'll put just his head around the edge
of the door to surprise us

Like this.

-Mewlana Jalaluddin Rumi

Light Up The Fire

I gaze into the heart, lowly it may be,
Thought the words be higher still.
For the heart is all the substance,
The speech an accident.
How many phrases will you speak,
Too many for me.
How much burning, burning will you feel,
Be friendly with the fire, enough for me.
Light up the fire of love inside,
And blaze the thoughts away.

-Mewlana Jalaluddin Rumi

Lord, what a Beloved is mine!

Lord, what a Beloved is mine! I have a sweet quarry; I possess
In my breast a hundred meadows from his reed.

When in anger the messenger comes and repairs towards me,
He says, "Whither are you fleeing? I have business with you."
Last night I asked the new moon concerning my Moon. The
Moon said, "I am running in his wake, my foot is in his dust."
When the sun arose I said," How yellow of face you are!" The
Sun said, "Out of shame for his countenance I have a face of
Gold."

"Water, you are prostrate, you are running on your head and
Face." Water said, "Because of his incantation I move like a
Snake."

"Noble fire, why do you writhe so?" Fire said, "Because of
The lightning of his face my heart is restless."

"Wind-messenger of the world, why are you light of heart?"
Wind said, "My heart would burn if the choice were mine."

"Earth, what are you meditation, silent and watchful?" Earth
Said, "Within me I have a garden and spring."

Pass over these elements, God is our succorer; my head is
Aching, in my hand I hold wine.

If you have barred sleep to us, the way of intoxication is open.
Since I have one to assist, he offers wine in both hands.

Be silent, that without this tongue the heart may speak; when
I hear the speech of the heart, I feel ashamed of this speech.

-Mewlana Jalaluddin Rumi

Love and imagination

Love and imagination are magicians
Who create an image of the Beloved in your mind
With which you share your secret intimate moments.
This apparition is made of nothing at al,
But from its mouth comes the question,
-Am I not your Loved One?'
and from you the soft reply'Yes.Yes.Yes.'

-Mewlana Jalaluddin Rumi

Love has nothing to do with the five senses

Love has nothing to do with
the five senses and the six directions:
its goal is only to experience
the attraction exerted by the Beloved.
Afterwards, perhaps, permission
will come from God:
the secrets that ought to be told will be told
with an eloquence nearer to the understanding
of these subtle confusing allusions.
The secret is partner with none
but the knower of the secret:
in the skeptic's ear
the secret is no secret at all.

-Mewlana Jalaluddin Rumi

Love is reckless

Love is reckless; not reason.
Reason seeks a profit.
Love comes on strong,
consuming herself, unabashed.

Yet, in the midst of suffering,
Love proceeds like a millstone,
hard surfaced and straightforward.

Having died of self-interest,
she risks everything and asks for nothing.
Love gambles away every gift God bestows.

Without cause God gave us Being;
without cause, give it back again.

-Mewlana Jalaluddin Rumi

Love Makes

Love makes bitter things sweet.
Love turns copper to gold.
With love dregs settle into clarity.
With love suffering ceases.
Love brings the dead back to life.
Love transforms the King into a slave.
Love is the consummation of Gnosis.
How could a fool sit on such a throne?

-Mewlana Jalaluddin Rumi

Love is the Water of Life

Everything other than love for the most beautiful
God

though it be sugar- eating.

What is agony of the spirit?

To advance toward death without seizing

hold of the Water of Life.

-Mewlana Jalaluddin Rumi

The Lovers

The Lovers
will drink wine night and day.
They will drink until they can
tear away the veils of intellect and
melt away the layers of shame and modesty.
When in Love,
body, mind, heart and soul don't even exist.
Become this,
fall in Love, and you will not be separated again.

-Mewlana Jalaluddin Rumi

Moving Water

When you do things from your soul, you feel a river
moving in you, a joy.

When actions come from another section, the feeling
disappears.

Don't let others lead you. They may be blind or, worse, vultures.

Reach for the rope of God. And what is that? Putting aside self-will.

Because of willfulness people sit in jail, the trapped bird's wings are
tied, fish sizzle in the skillet.

The anger of police is willfulness. You've seen a magistrate
inflict visible punishment.

Now see the invisible. If you could leave your selfishness, you
would see how you've been torturing your soul. We are born and
live inside black water in a well.

How could we know what an open field of sunlight is?

Don't insist on going where you think you want to go. Ask the way
to the spring. Your living pieces will form a harmony.

There is a moving palace that floats in the air with balconies and
clear water flowing through, infinity everywhere, yet contained
under a single tent.

-Mewlana Jalaluddin Rumi

Not Here

There's courage involved if you want
to become truth.

There is a broken- open place in a lover.

Where are those qualities of bravery and
sharp compassion in this group? What's the
use of old and frozen thought?

I want a howling hurt. This is not a treasury
where gold is stored; this is for copper.

We alchemists look for talent that
can heat up and change.

Lukewarm won't do. Halfhearted holding back,
well-enough getting by? Not here.

-Mewlana Jalaluddin Rumi

Not Intrigued With Evening

What the material world values does
not shine the same in the truth of the soul.

You have been interested
in your shadow. Look instead directly at the sun.

What can we know by just
watching the time-and-space shapes of each other?

Someone half awake in the night sees imaginary dangers;

the morning star rises; the horizon grows
defined; people become friends in a moving caravan.

Night birds may think
daybreak a kind of darkness, because
that's all they know.

It's a fortunate
bird who's not intrigued with evening,
who flies in the sun we call Shams.

-Mewlana Jalaluddin Rumi

O You Who've gone on Pilgrimage

O you who've gone on pilgrimage -
    where are you, where, oh where?
Here, here is the Beloved!
    Oh come now, come, oh come!
Your friend, he is your neighbor,
    he is next to your wall -
You, erring in the desert -
    what air of love is this?
If you'd see the Beloved's
    form without any form -
You are the house, the master,
    You are the Kaaba, you! . . .
Where is a bunch of roses,
    if you would be this garden?
Where, one soul's pearly essence
    when you're the Sea of God?
That's true - and yet your troubles
    may turn to treasures rich -
How sad that you yourself veil
    the treasure that is yours!

-Mewlana Jalaluddin Rumi

Ode 1373

I was dead, then alive.
Weeping, then laughing.

The power of love came into me,
and I became fierce like a lion,
then tender like the evening star.

He said, 'You're not mad enough.
You don't belong in this house.'

I went wild and had to be tied up.
He said, 'Still not wild enough
to stay with us!'

I broke through another layer
into joyfulness.

He said, 'Its not enough.'
I died.

He said, 'You are a clever little man,
full of fantasy and doubting.'

I plucked out my feathers and became a fool.
He said, 'Now you are the candle
for this assembly.'

But I'm no candle. Look!
I'm scattered smoke

-Mewlana Jalaluddin Rumi

He said, 'You are the Sheikh, the guide.'
But I'm not a teacher. I have no power.

He said, 'You already have wings.
I cannot give you wings.'

But I wanted his wings.
I felt like some flightless chicken.

Then new events said to me,
'Don't move. A sublime generosity is
coming towards you.'

And old love said, 'Stay with me.'

I said, 'I will.'

You are the fountain of the sun's light.
I am a willow shadow on the ground.
You make my raggedness silky.

The soul at dawn is like darkened water
that slowly begins to say Thank you, thank you.

Then at sunset, again, Venus gradually
Changes into the moon and then the whole nightsky.

This comes of smiling back
at your smile.

The chess master says nothing,
other than moving the silent chess piece.

That I am part of the ploys
of this game makes me
amazingly happy.

-Mewlana Jalaluddin Rumi

One Swaying Being

Love is not condescension, never
that, nor books, nor any marking
on paper, nor what people say of
each other. Love is a tree with
branches reaching into eternity
and roots set deep in eternity,
and no trunk! Have you seen it?
The mind cannot. Your desiring
cannot. The longing you feel for
this loves comes from inside you.
When you become the Friend, your
longing will be as the man in
the ocean who holds to a piece of
wood. Eventually, wood, man, and
oceans become one swaying being,

-Mewlana Jalaluddin Rumi

One Whisper Of The Beloved

Lovers share a sacred decree —
to seek the Beloved.
They roll head over heels,
rushing toward the Beautiful One
like a torrent of water.

In truth, everyone is a shadow of the Beloved —
Our seeking is His seeking,
Our words are His words.

At times we flow toward the Beloved
like a dancing stream.
At times we are still water
held in His pitcher.
At times we boil in a pot
turning to vapor —
that is the job of the Beloved.

He breathes into my ear
until my soul
takes on His fragrance.
He is the soul of my soul —
How can I escape?
But why would any soul in this world
want to escape from the Beloved?

He will melt your pride
making you thin as a strand of hair,
Yet do not trade, even for both worlds,
One strand of His hair.

We search for Him here and there
while looking right at Him.
Sitting by His side we ask,
'O Beloved, where is the Beloved?'

Enough with such questions! –
Let silence take you to the core of life.

All your talk is worthless
When compared to one whisper
of the Beloved.

-Mewlana Jalaluddin Rumi

Our Death Is Our Wedding With Eternity

Our death is our wedding with eternity.
What is the secret? 'God is One.'
The sunlight splits when entering the windows of the house.
This multiplicity exists in the cluster of grapes;
It is not in the juice made from the grapes.
For he who is living in the Light of God,
The death of the carnal soul is a blessing.
Regarding him, say neither bad nor good,
For he is gone beyond the good and the bad.
Fix your eyes on God and do not talk about what is invisible,
So that he may place another look in your eyes.
It is in the vision of the physical eyes
That no invisible or secret thing exists.
But when the eye is turned toward the Light of God
What thing could remain hidden under such a Light?
Although all lights emanate from the Divine Light
Don't call all these lights 'the Light of God';
It is the eternal light which is the Light of God,
The ephemeral light is an attribute of the body and the flesh.
...Oh God who gives the grace of vision!
The bird of vision is flying towards You with the wings of desire.

-Mewlana Jalaluddin Rumi

Out Beyond Ideas

Out beyond ideas of wrongdoing and rightdoing,
there is a field. I'll meet you there.

When the soul lies down in that grass,
the world is too full to talk about.
Ideas, language, even the phrase each other
doesn't make any sense

-Mewlana Jalaluddin Rumi

Out Of Your Love

Out of your love the fire of youth will rise.
In the chest, visions of the soul will rise.
If you are going to kill me, kill me, it is alright.
When the friend kills, a new life will rise.

-Mewlana Jalaluddin Rumi

Passion makes the old medicine new

Passion makes the old medicine new:
Passion lops off the bough of weariness.
Passion is the elixir that renews:
how can there be weariness
when passion is present?
Oh, don't sigh heavily from fatigue:
seek passion, seek passion, seek passion!

-Mewlana Jalaluddin Rumi

Reason Says Love Says

Reason says, " I will beguile him with the tongue."; Love says,
"Be silent. I will beguile him with the soul."
The soul says to the heart, "Go, do not laugh at me and
yourself.
What is there that is not his, that I may beguile him

thereby?"He is not sorrowful and anxious and seeking oblivion
that Imay beguile him with wine and a heavy measure.The
arrow of his glance needs not a bow that I should beguilethe
shaft of his gaze with a bow.He is not prisoner of the world,
fettered to this world of earth,that I should beguile him with
gold of the kingdom of the world.He is an angel, though in
form he is a man; he is not lustfulthat I should beguile him
with women.Angels start away from the house wherein this
form is, so howshould I beguile him with such a form and
likeness?

He does not take a flock of horses, since he flies on wings;
hisfood is light, so how should I beguile him with bread?He is
not a merchant and trafficker in the market of the worldthat I
should beguile him with enchantment of grain and loss.He is
not veiled that I should make myself out sick and uttersighs, to
beguile him with lamentation.

I will bind my head and bow my head, for I have got out
ofhand; I will not beguile his compassion with sickness or
fluttering.Hair by hair he sees my crookedness and feigning;
what'shidden from him that I should beguile him with
anything hidden.He is not a seeker of fame, a prince addicted
to poets, that Ishould beguile him with verses and lyrics and
flowing poetry.The glory of the unseen form is too great for
me to beguile itwith blessing or Paradise.Shams-e Tabriz, who
is his chosen and beloved—perchance Iwill beguile him with
this same pole of the age.

-Mewlana Jalaluddin Rumi

Shadow and Light Source Both

How does a part of the world leave the world?
How does wetness leave water?

Dont' try to put out fire by throwing on
more fire! Don't wash a wound with blood.

No matter how fast you run, your shadow
keeps up. Sometimes it's in front!

Only full overhead sun diminishes your shadow.
But that shadow has been serving you.

What hurts you, blesses you. Darkness is
your candle. Your boundaries are your quest.

I could explain this, but it will break the
glass cover on your heart, and there's no
fixing that.

You must have shadow and light source both.
Listen, and lay your head under the tree of awe.

When from that tree feathers and wings sprout on you,
be quieter than a dove. Don't even open your mouth for
even a coo.

-Mewlana Jalaluddin Rumi

Sleep of the Body the Soul's Awakening

Every night Thou freest our spirits from the body
And its snare, making them pure as rased tablets.
Every night spirits are released from this cage,
And set free, neither lording it nor lorded over.
At night prisoners are unaware of their prison,
At night kings are unaware of their majesty.
Then there is no thought or care for loss or gain,
No regard to such an one or such an one.
The state of the "Knower" is such as this, even when awake.
God says,4 "Thou wouldst deem him awake though asleep,
Sleeping to the affairs of the world, day and night,
Like a pen in the directing hand of the writer.
He who sees not the hand which effects the writing
Fancies the effect proceeds from the motion of the pen.
If the "Knower" revealed the particulars of this state,
'Twould rob the vulgar of their sensual sleep.
His soul wanders in the desert that has no similitude;
Like his body, his spirit is enjoying perfect rest;
Freed from desire of eating and drinking,
Like a bird escaped from cage and snare.
But when he is again beguiled into the snare,
He cries for help to the Almighty.

-Mewlana Jalaluddin Rumi

Soul Receives From Soul

Soul receives from soul that knowledge,
therefore not by book nor from tongue.

If knowledge of mysteries come after
emptiness of mind, that is illumination of heart.

-Mewlana Jalaluddin Rumi

That Lives In Us

If you put your hands on this oar with me,
they will never harm another,
and they will come to findthey hold everything you want.
If you put your hands on this oar with me,
they would no longer

lift anything to your
mouth that might wound your precious land-
that sacred earth that is
your body.

If you put your soul against this oar with me,
the power that made the universe will enter your sinew
from a source not outside your limbs, but from a holy realm
that lives in us.

Exuberant is existence, time a husk.
When the moment cracks open, ecstasy leaps out and devours
space;

love goes mad with the blessings, like my words give.
Why lay yourself on the torturer's rack of the past and future?
The mind that tries to shape tomorrow beyond its capacities
will find no rest.

Be kind to yourself, dear- to our innocent follies.
Forget any sounds or touch you knew that did not help you dance.
You will come to see that all evolves us.

If you put your heart against the earth with me, in serving
every creature, our Beloved will enter you from our sacred realm
and we will be, we will be
so happy.

-Mewlana Jalaluddin Rumi

The Agony And Ecstasy

In the orchard and rose garden
I long to see your face.
In the taste of Sweetness
I long to kiss your lips.
In the shadows of passion
I long for your love.
Oh! Supreme Lover!
Let me leave aside my worries.
The flowers are blooming
with the exultation of your Spirit.
By Allah!
I long to escape the prison of my ego
and lose myself
in the mountains and the desert.
These sad and lonely people tire me.
I long to revel in the drunken frenzy of your love
and feel the strength of Rustam in my hands.
I'm sick of mortal kings.
I long to see your light.
With lamps in hand
the sheiks and mullahs roam
the dark alleys of these towns
not finding what they seek.
You are the Essence of the Essence,
The intoxication of Love.
I long to sing your praises
but stand mute
with the agony of wishing in my heart.

-Mewlana Jalaluddin Rumi

The beauty of the heart

The beauty of the heart
is the lasting beauty:
its lips give to drink
of the water of life.
Truly it is the water,
that which pours,
and the one who drinks.
All three become one when
your talisman is shattered.
That oneness you can't know
by reasoning.

-Mewlana Jalaluddin Rumi

The Breeze at Dawn

The breeze at dawn has secrets to tell you.
Don't go back to sleep.

You must ask for what you really want.
Don't go back to sleep.

People are going back and forth across the doorsill
where the two worlds touch.

The door is round and open.
Don't go back to sleep.

-Mewlana Jalaluddin Rumi

The Chance Of Humming

A man
standing on two logs in a river
might do all right floating with the
current while humming in the
now.

Though
if one log is tied to a camel,
who is also heading south along the
bank - at the same pace-
all could still be well
with the world unless the camel
thinks he forgot something, and
abruptly turns upstream,
then uh-oh.

Most minds
do not live in the present
and can stick to a reasonable plan;
most minds abruptly turn
and undermine the
chance of humming.

-Mewlana Jalaluddin Rumi

The Meaning Of Love

Both light and shadow
are the dance of Love.
Love has no cause;
it is the astrolabe of God's secrets.
Lover and Loving are inseparable
and timeless.
Although I may try to describe Love
when I experience it I am speechless.
Although I may try to write about Love
I am rendered helpless;
my pen breaks and the paper slips away
at the ineffable place
where Lover, Loving and Loved are one.
Every moment is made glorious
by the light of Love.

-Mewlana Jalaluddin Rumi

The Privileged Lovers

The moon has become a dancer
at this festival of love.
This dance of light,

This sacred blessing,
This divine love,
beckons us
to a world beyond
only lovers can see
with their eyes of fiery passion.

They are the chosen ones
who have surrendered.
Once they were particles of light
now they are the radiant sun.

They have left behind
the world of deceitful games.
They are the privileged lovers
who create a new world
with their eyes of fiery passion.

-Mewlana Jalaluddin Rumi

The ravings which my enemy uttered I heard within my heart

The ravings which my enemy uttered I heard within my heart;
the secret thoughts he harbored against me I also perceived.
His dog bit my foot, he showed me much injustice; I do not
bite him like a dog, I have bitten my own lip.
Since I have penetrated into the secrets of individuals like men
of God, why should I take glory in having penetrated his secret?
I reproach myself that through my doubtings it so happened
that purposely I drew a scorpion towards my own foot.
Like Eblis who saw nothing of Adam except his fire, by God I
was invisible to his insignificant Eblis.
Convey to my friends why I am afflicted in mind; when the
snake bit my thigh I started away from the black rope.
The blessed silent ones, their lips and eyes closed –by a way
unknown to any man, I ran into their thoughts;
Since there is a secret and perfect way from heart to heart, I
gathered gold and silver from the treasuries of hearts.
Into the thought that was like a brazen stove I flung the dead
dog; out of the thought that was like a rose bower I plucked roses
and jasmine.
If I have hinted at the evil and good of my friends, I have spun
flax like a weaver as the choicest veil.
When my heart rushed suddenly to a heart mighty and aware,
out of awe for his heart I fluttered like the heart.
As you are happy with your own state, how did you fall in with
me? Attend to your own business, for I am neither shaikh nor
disciple.
As far as you are concerned, brother, I am neither copper nor
red gold; drive me from your door, for I am neither lock nor key.
Take it as if I had not ever spoken these words; if you had been
in my mind, by God I would not have quarreled.

-Mewlana Jalaluddin Rumi

The Seed Market

Can you find another market like this?
Where,
with your one rose
you can buy hundreds of rose gardens?
Where,
for one seed
get a whole wilderness?
For one weak breath,
a divine wind?
You've been fearful
of being absorbed in the ground,
or drawn up by the air.
Now, your waterbead lets go
and drops into the ocean,
where it came from.
It no longer has the form it had,
but it's still water
The essence is the same.
This giving up is not a repenting.
It's a deep honoring of yourself.
When the ocean comes to you as a lover,
marry at once, quickly,
for God's sake!
Don't postpone it!
Existence has no better gift.
No amount of searching
will find this.
A perfect falcon, for no reason
has landed on your shoulder,
and become yours.

-Mewlana Jalaluddin Rumi

The Self We Share

Thirst is angry with water. Hunger bitter
with bread.

The cave wants nothing to do with the sun.

This is dumb, the self- defeating way
we've been.

A gold mine is calling us into its temple.
Instead, we bend and keep picking up rocks
from the ground.

Every thing has a shine like gold,
but we should turn to the source!

The origin is what we truly are. I add a little
vinegar to the honey I give.

The bite of scolding makes ecstasy more familiar.

But look, fish, you're already in the ocean:
just swimming there makes you friends with
glory.

What are these grudges about? You are Benjamin.
Joseph has put a gold cup in your grain sack and
accused you of being a thief.

-Mewlana Jalaluddin Rumi

Now he draws you aside and says,
'You are my brother. I

am a prayer. You're the amen.'

We move in eternal regions, yet
worry about property here.

This is the prayer of each:

You are the source of my life.
You separate essence from mud.

You honor my soul. You bring rivers from the
mountain springs. You brighten my eyes.

The wine you offer takes me out of myself into
the self we share. Doing that is religion.

-Mewlana Jalaluddin Rumi

The springtime of Lovers has come

The springtime of Lovers has come,
that this dust bowl may become a garden;
the proclamation of heaven has come,
that the bird of the soul may rise in flight.
The sea becomes full of pearls,
the salt marsh becomes sweet as kauthar,
the stone becomes a ruby from the mine,
the body becomes wholly soul.

-Mewlana Jalaluddin Rumi

The Taste of Morning

Time's knife slides from the sheath,
as fish from where it swims.

Being closer and closer is the desire
of the body. Don't wish for union!

There's a closeness beyond that. Why
would God want a second God? Fall in

love in such a way that it frees you
from any connecting. Love is the soul's

light, the taste of morning, no me, no
we, no claim of being. These words

are the smoke the fire gives off as it
absolves its defects, as eyes in silence,

tears, face. Love cannot be said.

-Mewlana Jalaluddin Rumi

The Temple Of Love

The temple of love is not love itself;
True love is the treasure,
Not the walls about it.
Do not admire the decoration,
But involve yourself in the essence,
The perfume that invades and touches you—
The beginning and the end.
Discovered, this replace all else,
The apparent and the unknowable.
Time and space are slaves to this presence.

-Mewlana Jalaluddin Rumi

The Way Things Should

What will
our children do in the morning?
Will they wake with their hearts wanting to play,
the way wings should?
Will they have dreamed the needed flights and
gathered
the strength from the planets that all
men and women need to balance
the wonderful charms of
the earth
so that her power and beauty does not make us
forget our own?
I know all about the ways of the heart – how it
wants to be alive.
Love so needs to love
that it will endure almost anything, even abuse,
just to flicker for a moment. But the sky's mouth is
kind,
its song will never hurt you, for I sing those words.
What will our children do in the morning
if they do not see us
fly?

-Mewlana Jalaluddin Rumi

There Are A Hundred Kinds Of Prayer

Today, like every day, we are ruined, ruined (by "wine").

Don't open the door of worry, but take up the lute!

There are a hundred kinds of prayer, bowing, and prostration6

For the one whose prayer-niche, is the beauty of the Beloved

-**Mewlana Jalaluddin Rumi**

There is a Candle in your Heart

There is a candle in the heart of man, waiting to be kindled.
In separation from the Friend, there is a cut waiting to be
stitched.

O, you who are ignorant of endurance and the burning
fire of love—

Love comes of its own free will, it can't be learned
in any school.

-Mewlana Jalaluddin Rumi

There is a life-force within your soul

There is a life-force within your soul, seek that life.
There is a gem in the mountain of your body, seek that
mine.
O traveler, if you are in search of That
Don't look outside, look inside yourself and seek That.

-Mewlana Jalaluddin Rumi

There is a Community of Spirit

There is a community of the spirit.
Join it, and feel the delight
of walking in the noisy street
and being the noise.
Drink all your passion,
and be a disgrace.
Close both eyes
to see with the other eye.

-Mewlana Jalaluddin Rumi

There Is A Way

There is a way between voice and presence
where information flows.
In disciplined silence it opens.
With wandering talk it closes.

-Mewlana Jalaluddin Rumi

This Aloneness

This aloneness is worth more than a thousand lives.
This freedom is worth more than all the lands on earth.
To be one with the truth for just a moment,
Is worth more than the world and life itself.

-Mewlana Jalaluddin Rumi

This Is Love

This is love: to fly toward a secret sky,
to cause a hundred veils to fall each moment.
First, to let go of live.

In the end, to take a step without feet;
to regard this world as invisible,
and to disregard what appears to be the self.

Heart, I said, what a gift it has been
to enter this circle of lovers,
to see beyond seeing itself,
to reach and feel within the breast.

-Mewlana Jalaluddin Rumi

This we Have Now

This we have now
is not imagination.

This is not
grief or joy.

Not a judging state,
or an elation,
or sadness.

Those come and go.
This is the presence that doesn't.

-Mewlana Jalaluddin Rumi

This Will Not Win Him

Reason says,
I will win him with my eloquence.

Love says,
I will win him with my silence.

Soul says,
How can I ever win him
When all I have is already his?

He does not want, he does not worry,
He does not seek a sublime state of euphoria -
How then can I win him
With sweet wine or gold?

He is not bound by the senses -
How then can I win him
With all the riches of China?

He is an angel,
Though he appears in the form of a man.
Even angels cannot fly in his presence -
How then can I win him
By assuming a heavenly form?

He flies on the wings of God,
His food is pure light -
How then can I win him
With a loaf of baked bread?

-Mewlana Jalaluddin Rumi

He is neither a merchant, nor a tradesman -
How then can I win him
With a plan of great profit?

He is not blind, nor easily fooled -
How then can I win him
By lying in bed as if gravely ill?

I will go mad, pull out my hair,
Grind my face in the dirt -
How will this win him?

He sees everything -
how can I ever fool him?

He is not a seeker of fame,
A prince addicted to the praise of poets -
How then can I win him
With flowing rhymes and poetic verses?

The glory of his unseen form
Fills the whole universe
How then can I win him
With a mere promise of paradise?

I may cover the earth with roses,
I may fill the ocean with tears,
I may shake the heavens with praises -
none of this will win him.

There is only one way to win him,
this Beloved of mine -

Become his.

-Mewlana Jalaluddin Rumi

Two Friends

A certain person came to the Friend's door
and knocked.
"Who's there?"
"It's me."

The Friend answered, "Go away. There's no place
for raw meat at this table."

The individual went wandering for a year.
Nothing but the fire of separation
can change hypocrisy and ego.
The person returned
completely cooked,
walked up and down in front of the Friend's house,
gently knocked.
"Who is it?"
"You."

"Please come in, my self,
there's no place in this house for two.
The doubled end of the thread is not what goes through
the eye of the needle.

It's a single-pointed, fined-down, thread end,
not a big ego-beast with baggage."

-Mewlana Jalaluddin Rumi

Two Kinds of Intelligence

There are two kinds of intelligence: one acquired,
as a child in school memorizes facts and concepts
from books and from what the teacher says,
collecting information from the traditional sciences
as well as from the new sciences.

With such intelligence you rise in the world.
You get ranked ahead or behind others
in regard to your competence in retaining
information. You stroll with this intelligence
in and out of fields of knowledge, getting always more
marks on your preserving tablets.

There is another kind of tablet, one
already completed and preserved inside you.
A spring overflowing its springbox. A freshness
in the center of the chest. This other intelligence
does not turn yellow or stagnate. It's fluid,
and it doesn't move from outside to inside
through conduits of plumbing-learning.

This second knowing is a fountainhead
from within you, moving out.

-Mewlana Jalaluddin Rumi

Until You've Found Pain

Until you've found pain, you won't reach the cure
Until you've given up life, you won't unite with
the supreme soul
Until you've found fire inside yourself, like the Friend,
You won't reach the spring of life, like Khezr.

-Mewlana Jalaluddin Rumi

Untitled

The minute I heard my first love story
I started looking for you, not knowing
how blind that was.
Lovers don't finally meet somewhere
They're in each other all along.

-Mewlana Jalaluddin Rumi

We Are As The Flute

We are as the flute, and the music in us is from thee;
we are as the mountain and the echo in us is from thee.

We are as pieces of chess engaged in victory and defeat:
our victory and defeat is from thee,
O thou whose qualities are comely!

Who are we, O Thou soul of our souls,
that we should remain in being beside thee?

We and our existences are really non-existence;
thou art the absolute Being which manifests the perishable.

We all are lions, but lions on a banner:
because of the wind they are rushing
onward from moment to moment.

Their onward rush is visible,
and the wind is unseen:
may that which is unseen not fail from us!

Our wind whereby we are moved and our being are of thy gift;
our whole existence is from thy bringing into being.

-Mewlana Jalaluddin Rumi

Weary Not Of Us, For We Are Very Beautiful

Weary not of us, for we are very beautiful; it is out of very jealousy
and proper pride that we entered the veil.

On the day when we cast of the body-s veil from the soul, you will
see that we are the envy of despair of man and the Polestars.

Wash your face and become clean for beholding us, else remain
afar, for we are beloveds of ourselves.

We are not that beauty who tomorrow will become a crone; till
eternity we are young and heart-comforting and fair of stature.

If that veil become worn out, the beauty has not grown old; the life
of the Veil is transient, and we are boundless life.

When Eblis saw the veil of Adam, he refused; Adam called to him, -
You are the rejected one, not I.â?◼

The rest of the angels fell down prostrate, saying as they bowed
themselves, -We have encountered a beauty:

-Beneath the veil is an idol who by his qualities robbed us of reason,
and we, prostrate, fell.â?◼

If our reason does not know the forms of the foul old men from
those of the beauties, we are apostates from love.

What place is there for a beauty? For he is the Lion of God. Like a
child we prattled, for we are children of the alphabet.

Children are beguiled with nuts and raisins, else, how are we meet
for nuts and sesame-grains?

When an old woman is hidden in helmet and chainmail, she says, -I
am the illustrious Rostam of the battle ranks.â?◼

By her boast all know that she is a woman; how should we make a
mistake, seeing that we are in the light of Ahmad?

-The believer is discriminatingâ?◼ - so said the Prophet; now close
your mouth, for we are guided rightly without speech.

Hear the rest of from Shams the Pride of Tabiz for we did not take
the end of the story from that king.

-Mewlana Jalaluddin Rumi

What Hidden Sweetness Is There

What hidden sweetness there is in this emptiness of the belly!
Man is surely like a lute, no more and no less;
For if, for instance, the belly of the lute becomes full, no
lament high or low will arise from that full lute.
If your brain and belly are on fire through fasting, because of
the fire every moment a lament will arise from your breast.
Every moment you will burn a thousand veils by that fire; you
will mount a hundred steps with zeal and endeavor.
Become empty of belly, and weep entreatingly like the reed
pipe; become empty of belly, and tell secrets with the reed pen.
If your belly is full at the time of concourse, it will bring Satan
in place of your reason, an idol in place of the Kaaba.
When you keep the fast, good habits gather together before
you like slaves and servants and retinue.
Keep the fast, for that is Solomon's ring; give not the ring to
the div, destroy not your kingdom.
Even if your kingdom has gone from your head and your army
has fled, your army will rise up, pennants flying above them.
The table arrived from heaven to the tents of the fast, by the
intervention of the prayers of Jesus, son of Mary.
In the fast, be expectant of the table of bounty, for the table of
bounty is better than the broth of cabbages.

-**Mewlana Jalaluddin Rumi**

What Was Told, That

What was said to the rose that made it open was said
to me here in my chest.

What was told the cypress that made it strong

and straight, what was

whispered the jasmine so it is what it is, whatever made
sugarcane sweet, whatever

was said to the inhabitants of the town of Chigil in
Turkestan that makes them

so handsome, whatever lets the pomegranate flower blush
like a human face, that is

being said to me now. I blush. Whatever put eloquence in
language, that's happening here.

The great warehouse doors open; I fill with gratitude,
chewing a piece of sugarcane,

in love with the one to whom every that belongs!

-Mewlana Jalaluddin Rumi

When Grapes Turn To Wine

When grapes turn
to wine, they long for our ability to change.

When stars wheel
around the North Pole,
they are longing for our growing consciousness.

Wine got drunk with us,
not the other way.
The body developed out of us, not we from it.

We are bees,
and our body is a honeycomb.
We made
the body, cell by cell we made it.

-Mewlana Jalaluddin Rumi

When I am asleep and crumbling in the tomb

When I am asleep and crumbling in the tomb, should you come
to visit me, I will come forth with speed.
You are for me the blast of the trumpet and the resurrection,
so what shall I do? Dead or living, wherever you are, there am I.
Without your lip I am a frozen and silent reed; what melodies
I play the moment you breathe on my reed!
Your wretched reed has become accustomed to your sugar lip;
remember wretched me, for I am seeking you.
When I do not find the moon of your countenance, I bind up
my head [veil myself in your mourning]; when I do not find your
sweet lip, gnaw my own hand.

-Mewlana Jalaluddin Rumi

When I Die

When I die
when my coffin
is being taken out
you must never think
i am missing this world

don't shed any tears
don't lament or
feel sorry
i'm not falling
into a monster's abyss

when you see
my corpse is being carried
don't cry for my leaving
i'm not leaving
i'm arriving at eternal love

when you leave me
in the grave
don't say goodbye
remember a grave is
only a curtain
for the paradise behind

you'll only see me
descending into a grave
now watch me rise
how can there be an end
when the sun sets or
the moon goes down

it looks like the end
it seems like a sunset
but in reality it is a dawn
when the grave locks you up
that is when your soul is freed

have you ever seen
a seed fallen to earth
not rise with a new life
why should you doubt the rise
of a seed named human

have you ever seen
a bucket lowered into a well
coming back empty
why lament for a soul
when it can come back
like Joseph from the well

when for the last time
you close your mouth
your words and soul
will belong to the world of
no place no time

-Mewlana Jalaluddin Rumi

When The Rose Is Gone

When the rose is gone and the garden faded
you will no longer hear the nightingale's song.
The Beloved is all; the lover just a veil.
The Beloved is living; the lover a dead thing.
If love withholds its strengthening care,
the lover is left like a bird without care,
the lover is left like a bird without wings.
How will I be awake and aware
if the light of the Beloved is absent?
Love wills that this Word be brought forth

-Mewlana Jalaluddin Rumi

Who is at my door?

He said, "Who is at my door?"
I said, "Your humble servant."
He said, "What business do you have?"
I said, "To greet you, o Lord."

He said, "How long will you journey on?"
I said, "Until you stop me."
He said, "How long will you boil in the fire?"
I said, "Until I am pure.

"This is my oath of love.
For the sake of love
I gave up wealth and position."

He said, "You have pleaded your case
but you have no witness."
I said, "My tears are my witness;
the pallor of my face is my proof.'
He said, "Your witness has no credibility;
your eyes are too wet to see."
I said, "By the splendor of your justice
my eyes are clear and faultless."

He said, "What do you seek?"
I said, "To have you as my constant friend."
He said, "What do you want from me?"
I said, "Your abundant grace."

He said, "Who was your companion on the journey?
I said, "The thought of you, o King."
He said, "What called you here?"
I said, "The fragrance of your wine."

He said, "What brings you the most fulfillment?"
I said, "The company of the Emperor."
He said, "What do you find there?"
I said, "A hundred miracles."
He said, "Why is the palace deserted?"
I said, "They all fear the thief."
He said, "Who is the thief?"
I said, "The one who keeps me from -you.

He said, "Where is there safety?"
I said, "In service and renunciation."
He said, "What is there to renounce?"
I said, "The hope of salvation."

He said, "Where is there calamity?"
I said, "In the presence of your love."
He said, "How do you benefit from this life?"
I said, "By keeping true to myself

Now it is time for silence.
If I told you about His true essence
You would fly from your self and be gone,
and neither door nor roof could hold you back!

-Mewlana Jalaluddin Rumi

Who makes these changes?

Who makes these changes?
I shoot an arrow right.
It lands left.
I ride after a deer and find myself
Chased by a hog.
I plot to get what I want
And end up in prison.
I dig pits to trap others
And fall in.

I should be suspicious
Of what I want.

-Mewlana Jalaluddin Rumi

Who Says Words With My Mouth?

All day I think about it, then at night I say it.
Where did I come from, and what am I supposed to be doing?
I have no idea.
My soul is from elsewhere, I'm sure of that,
and I intend to end up there.

This drunkenness began in some other tavern.
When I get back around to that place,
I'll be completely sober. Meanwhile,
I'm like a bird from another continent, sitting in this aviary.
The day is coming when I fly off,
but who is it now in my ear who hears my voice?
Who says words with my mouth?

Who looks out with my eyes? What is the soul?
I cannot stop asking.
If I could taste one sip of an answer,
I could break out of this prison for drunks.
I didn't come here of my own accord, and I can't leave that way.
Whoever brought me here will have to take me home.

This poetry, I never know what I'm going to say.
I don't plan it.
When I'm outside the saying of it,
I get very quiet and rarely speak at all.

-Mewlana Jalaluddin Rumi

Whoever Brought Me Here

All day I think about it, then at night I say it.
Where did I come from, and what am I supposed to be doing?
I have no idea.
My soul is from elsewhere, I'm sure of that,
and I intend to end up there.

This drunkenness began in some other tavern.
When I get back around to that place,
I'll be completely sober. Meanwhile,
I'm like a bird from another continent, sitting in this aviary.
The day is coming when I fly off,
but who is it now in my ear who hears my voice?
Who says words with my mouth?

Who looks out with my eyes? What is the soul?
I cannot stop asking.
If I could taste one sip of an answer,
I could break out of this prison for drunks.
I didn't come here of my own accord, and I can't leave that way.
Whoever brought me here, will have to take me home.

This poetry. I never know what I'm going to say.
I don't plan it.
When I'm outside the saying of it,
I get very quiet and rarely speak at all.

-Mewlana Jalaluddin Rumi

With Passion

With
passion pray. With
passion work. With passion make love.
With passion eat and drink and dance and play.
Why look like a dead fish
in this ocean
of
God?

-Mewlana Jalaluddin Rumi

You Personify God's Message

You personify God's message.
You reflect the King's face.
There is nothing in the universe that you are not
Everything you want, look for it within yourself—
you are that.

-Mewlana Jalaluddin Rumi

Your grief....

Your grief for what you've lost holds a mirror
up to where you're bravely working.

Expecting the worst, you look and instead,
here's the joyful face you've been wanting to see.

Your hand opens and closes and opens and closes.
If it were always a fist or always stretched open,
you would be paralyzed.

Your deepest presence is in every small contracting and expand
the two as beautifully balanced and coordinated
as birdwings.

-Mewlana Jalaluddin Rumi

Zero Circle

Be helpless, dumbfounded,
Unable to say yes or no.
Then a stretcher will come from grace
To gather us up.

We are too dull-eyed to see that beauty
If we say we can, we're lying.
If we say No, we don't see it,
That No will behead us
And shut tight our window onto spirit.

So let us rather not be sure of anything,
Besides ourselves, and only that, so
Miraculous beings come running to help.
Crazed, lying in a zero circle, mute,
We shall be saying finally,

With tremendous eloquence, Lead us.
When we have totally surrendered to that beauty,
We shall be a mighty kindness.

-Mewlana Jalaluddin Rumi

About Author

Burhan Unver is a poet and author of the bestselling Rumi and Shams Quotes. He lives in Konya. Konya is truly one of the most spiritual cities in the world, dating back to the period of Rumi, Shams and their beautiful spiritual beliefs. For other books please check out the Burhan Unver's author page.

Made in the USA
Columbia, SC
27 November 2021

49843192R00059